5

SECRETS

— TO —

PERSONAL
PRODUCTIVITY

D1456857

BY KURT HANKS AND
GERRELD L. PULSIPHER

Franklin Quest Co.
P.O. Box 25127
Salt Lake City, Utah 84125-0127

Printed in the United States of America

ISBN# 0-939817-05-5

Table of Contents

ONE

3-Minute MEMORY METHOD

A simple way to learn and remember anything better, faster, and more permanently.

If you've ever wanted to be able to recall a particular gem of wisdom, an insightful idea gleaned from reading, or the key points made in a powerful presentation . . . If you've tried to store such things away in your mind for future reference, only to lose them somewhere in that mass of gray matter . . . Read on!

Franklin's 3-Minute Memory Method:

- Can help you retain any kind of information you want to store in your brain, ready for recall as needed

- Will enable you to do it in an easy and simple manner, without special devices, tricks, or hocus-pocus

- Uses your Franklin Day Planner as a tool to make the storing process happen automatically

- Utilizes the natural mental processes and methods your mind uses to store and relate information

- Will achieve sizable improvements in your retention for a small investment in time

NOTE: Boxes like these will appear on subsequent articles in this book. Later in this section we'll explain what the boxes are and how to use them.

How Your Memory Works

The brain's normal, information-sorting process involves two major storage centers—short-term memory and long-term memory. Each type of memory plays its special role in the sorting and filing process.

Short-Term Memory

Any incoming information first goes to the short-term memory. It all goes there for processing—such diverse input as the smell of today's lunchtime enchilada, the pep talk you heard in the sales meeting this morning, the programs and commercials you saw on T.V., the chirp of the crickets outside the window tonight, the itchy feeling of the new sweater.

As it comes in, the brain immediately processes the information, searching for any items that might be of life-sustaining importance. These are handled on a top-priority basis so that your body can act accordingly. Many irrelevant stimuli are discarded almost immediately, and the remainder go into the short-term memory. There they are automatically dropped from consciousness after a few days. Unless we make a conscious effort to work with recently received information, we lose conscious recall of 80 percent of it within 24 hours and almost all of it within a few days.

We lose most of what we learn within 24 hours.

Benefits: This natural screening process helps us avoid being swamped by irrelevant data or distracting information. Having instant recall of all incoming information might make us a winner at *Trivial Pursuit*, but we'd spend a lot of mental energy sorting out which times in our minds were important and which weren't.

Disadvantages: There can be problems with the short-term memory's automatic discarding methods. The short-term memory can discard the important as easily as the trivial. Thus, we too easily forget critical information, or we find ourselves frequently having to relearn the same material we have gone through earlier.

Long-Term Memory

Fortunately, those impressions of greatest impact on us and the information that we consciously seek to retain are usually transferred from our short-term memory to our long-term memory banks. That's where we find our childhood memories and our working body of things we've mastered through practice or intuition—math skills, language, communication skills, and other skills. And, we'll find file after file of knowledge acquired through our years of formal and informal education.

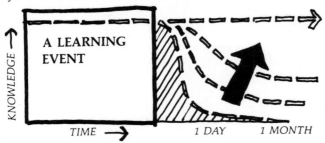

Systematic recall of information increases our retention of it.

Accomplishing the Memory Shift

The move from short- to long-term memory is most easily accomplished when there's a strong emotional association with the information (remember your first kiss?), when it's unique or strange, or when it is associated with some critical need we have. That's why some memory-expansion systems use weird imagery to help you remember information.

Even when there is no emotional tie, nothing unique or strange, or no critical need associated with the information, we can still make the transfer through repetition—gradually imprinting the information on our long-term consciousness. This is the way we're usually taught to memorize—a long, boring process most of us have little desire to undertake.

A Better Way . . .

There's another way to make a memory shift—a simple, fast, and effective method based on the latest findings about how the mind works. This method is centered on a key concept:

By identifying an overall pattern to the information and progressively reviewing the pattern at a rapid rate, you can shift the information from your short-term memory to your long-term memory.

The 3-Minute Memory Method

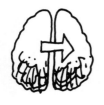

Right Brain and Left Brain: There's a Difference

The left brain is used when we initially read and understand the words; the right brain identifies the larger patterns and helps imprint them.

What It Is:

To transfer information from short-term to long-term memory, you identify key words and patterns in the information and then scan it five times over the next year. After the initial reading of the information, the entire process generally requires only about three minutes total elapsed time over that period to transfer the information permanently.

Why It Works:

Researchers are finding that the principal way the mind processes information is through images—we think in pictures, not words. Words are devices that we use to represent commonly shared images and to communicate with other people, but the brain translates words into images for its own processing and translates images back into words for verbal communication.

Because the brain works in images and patterns, it also has the ability to see and identify the patterns in a piece of information very quickly. In a magazine article, for example, a few moments working with the material will quickly reveal a graphic layout pattern or key words and ideas that can be marked or extracted to create a pattern that the mind can remember.

Then, by repeatedly scanning the pattern, it can be permanently imprinted in the neurological patterns among the cells in the portion of the brain that stores our memory. Each time the pattern is mentally repeated, those neurological bonds are strengthened and made more permanent.

Doing It—as Easy as Checking a Box

The grouping of six boxes you saw on the first page of this report is a tool that will help you review any desired material on a systematic basis. The method is simple:

Read the material, then:

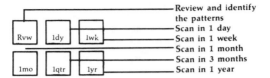

Here's How the 3-Minute Memory Method Works:

1: Read the Material

You're doing this already—reading articles and information pertaining to your interests or needs. When you find an article, talk, or idea particularly applicable to you, ask: Is this something I want to place in my long-term memory? If so, proceed to the next step.

2: Review Immediately

While the information is fresh in your mind, take a minute to review it. Mark or note key words or ideas that seem to lie at the heart of the information you want to retain. Let your mind use its natural abilities to identify patterns and organize the material in the way that seems to fit best. You'll find that this review and patterning process will go quickly—often done in as little as one minute.

To start the review process, draw the series of six boxes at the top of the sheet or apply one of the gummed labels with the boxes printed on them that are available from Franklin. Write today's date on the line above the boxes and check off the first box, "Rvw."

Now, place the article between tomorrow's pages in your Franklin Day Planner or make a note on your task list, where it will automatically come to your attention.

3: Scan on a Regular Schedule

The hard part's done at this point. Tomorrow, the article will automatically come to your attention for scanning, along with all of the other items you want to accomplish that day. Take 30 seconds or so to scan the patterns you've identified in the article, then check off the "1dy" box and move the article to the Day Planner page for one week from now.

Each time the article surfaces in your Day Planner, simply scan it, check off the appropriate box, and move it on to the next review point—one month, one quarter, or a year down the road.

NOTE: Don't worry about the seeming superficiality of the scanning process. The logical left half of your brain will protest that it doesn't make sense to do it this way, that it can't be this easy. But the scanning process uses other parts of the brain that will absorb and process this "booster" review almost subliminally.

Tips to Remember

The Review Step Is Critical

The most important step in the process is the review of the material after you initially read or receive the information. While all the information is fresh in your short-term memory, is the easiest time for your mind to identify the visual and structural patterns that help the 3-Minute Memory Method work.

For your first exercise, use the information contained on the previous four pages of this article. Make a photo copy of these pages. Circle the bold subtitles and the illustration of the six boxes and underline anything else that impressed you.

Other patterns you may wish to remember are the graphs and supporting material on pages 2 and 3 contrasting usual short-term memory loss with the longer retention possible when the information is systematically recalled and worked with. In addition, underline, mark, or annotate other ideas or information that impressed you.

When you have completed this brief review, check off the "Rvw" box on page 5, fold the sheet in half, punch holes, and place the article between tomorrow's pages in your Franklin Day Planner—and you'll have the process started.

Let Your Day Planner Remember

After you complete the initial review and patterning of the material, you can literally forget about it. Your Day Planner will pick up the process, and you need only concern yourself with a quick scanning of the material when it next surfaces in your Day Planner.

Quick Means Quick

When we say "quick," we mean just that. When you scan the material, you'll be looking at familiar information your brain has already processed once. The scanning process merely brings it to mind and quickly runs through it to help in imprinting.

This kind of scanning uses the pattern-oriented right half of your brain. It can process the information rapidly, so there's no need for laboriously plodding through all the words again. A typical scan of an article should take no more than 30 seconds.

It May Seem Strange at First

In the beginning, the logical part of your brain will think you're nuts—learning isn't supposed to be this easy, at least when measured against the way we've learned things over a lifetime.

We urge you to suspend judgment. Give the system and the parts of the brain it works with a chance to do their thing. As your success with the 3-Minute Memory Method becomes a cumulative part of your experience, your logical side will react favorably.

Scan at the Suggested Intervals

The importance of scanning the material at the times indicated cannot be overemphasized. Research indicates that the mind needs a "booster" on the information at these intervals in order to place it on a permanent file.

The Method Will Work with Anything

While we've emphasized the processing of printed information, the 3-Minute Memory Method will work with any form of information input. Magazine articles can be photocopied, folded, and carried in your Day Planner. Printed materials too bulky for the Day Planner can be numbered and filed sequentially, with a note to review them made on the appropriate pages in the Day Planner. In the case of material heard in talks and presentations, or

The entire time spent scanning will amount to only three minutes — the time it takes to cook an egg.

ideas that you develop through your own mental processes, make notes and organize the notes into patterns during the review step.

Entire books require a little more time in the review process to identify the basic patterns and key ideas underlying the informational instruction of the book. For example, a few minutes spent after reading the book *Megatrends* will quickly enable you to identify the key points to remember about each of author John Naisbitt's ten "trends that are changing our lives."

Try It!

The 3-Minute Memory Method has the potential to increase the productive processing, storing, and retrieving of information significantly. But it won't work until you implement it in your own life.

Knowledge without actual implementation is of no use.

We urge you to use the pages you copied from this article as a test. If you've already done the review of the material suggested on page 6, you need only check the "review" box and place the sheet between tomorrow's pages in your Franklin Day Planner. If you haven't yet reviewed the material, take a minute and do so now to get the test started.

If fully implemented in your life, the 3-Minute Memory Method can greatly increase your personal effectiveness.

The following concepts are presented in an easy and entertaining format, but they deal with fundamental perceptions that help explain many of the most common human relations difficulties. By understanding this simple concept, you will have a powerful tool that will help you understand and deal with people more effectively.

TWO

THE BELIEF WINDOW

Rvw	1dy	1wk
1mo	1qtr	1yr

A conceptual tool for reading motivations, predicting reactions, and directing yourself and others toward needed change.

- Now, after 30 years of marriage, I can explain why she has been acting that way all these years.
- The other members of the team couldn't believe my foresight when I accurately predicted what each of them would do in the sales meeting.
- I used to feel like I was talking to the wind, but now I seem to have much more impact with my teenagers.
- It gave me some incredible insights into the company's problems—it's even caused changes in my own thinking.
- As a salesman, I can clearly see now the difference between those sales I closed and those I didn't.
- The -*&^^$* idea works!

If you would like to know more, please turn the page.

Announcing a Unique Discovery

Out in front of every person is a large window through which he or she sees the world. It is invisible to all but the trained eye. And written on each window (by its owner) is a series of explanations, guides, or principles which direct the owner's behavior.

The better you can see what is written on an individual's belief window, the more you can predict future responses, explain past actions, and motivate needed changes.

Shown here is a belief window made visible:

THE BELIEF WINDOW — each one is unique to the individual.

Every window is firmly fastened to the person's head.

How and what the person sees through the window is determined by the principles they have written on the glass.

Your typical average person

The belief window is a naturally occurring phenomenon for all humans. Everyone, from your nephew to the President of the United States, has an individually con-structed window hanging out in front of them. And their lives are consistent with what they have written on the panes of glass.

How the Discovery Was Made

It came during a time I was working with a millionaire. I had worked with him on an occasional basis for years. Over all this time, he had exhibited a lot of very strange behavior. In the early years, before he had made his money, we just thought he was weird, and when he became rich he was viewed as eccentric. With a laugh and a shrug, people he worked with would explain his sometimes strange behavior as a result of sunspot activity or tight shorts.

Then, while attending a meeting with this man, I saw the reason for his strange behavior. It was a meeting where I didn't have to do anything but be there; my body needed to fill a chair, but my mind could be on Mars. As the meeting progressed, I suddenly had a flash of insight. I could see his belief window—just like it was sticking out in front of his face.

By being able to read the principle on his belief window, I saved myself from economic disaster.

And I could also see one of the principles written on the window: MY way is the RIGHT way, and I see things absolutely correctly.

The invisible had suddenly become visible. I could see the future and the disasters that would be mine if I continued to work with him. I could also see the past and the thread that tied those years of erratic behavior together into a coherent pattern.

Belief windows are often invisible or hard to see, but they are a common characteristic of us all.

Put yourself in my shoes, and you can see the power of understanding that single principle on that person's belief window: If a person who has bought that principle were to join you in a business venture and the business failed, whose fault would he feel it to have been—his, or yours? In a disagreement over management, marketing directions, or anything, who would have the only correct view? As long as that principle was written on his belief window, could you ever possibly come out on top?

Having that insight was a lifesaver for me economically. After realizing that the patterns of his behavior were all consistent with the principle, I broke off my business association with the man. Later, I warned others who were involved with this person. Several said, "Don't get all worked up. Things are going to work out just fine. You've got to be crazy not to go in with us."

The ability to read others' belief windows (and our own) is one of the most essential skills we can develop.

Half a year later the words were, "How I wish I had listened to you. I thought you were nuts, but I was the one who was crazy. It's one thing to lose a good deal of money if you're wealthy like him, but it is another if you are not."

Since discovering that first belief window, I've seen them on just about everyone. Being aware of other people's windows (and my own) has proved to be an essential tool in all my dealings with them.

More Thoughts about Belief Windows:

- A belief window defines what we do or don't do—what we see or don't see.
- Our individual needs provide the power. The principles written on our window direct that power.
- We are constantly scanning our environment through the window for specific satisfactions to our wants.
- The things written on the glass include our prejudices.
- We cannot behave inconsistently with our belief window. Our window controls our decisions.
- We consider what is written on our glass to be absolutely true, with no possible alternative.

Everyone has an individually constructed window.

Written on the window are Guiding Principles.

The windows can be made out of any material the person desires.

Those principles we have bought and continue to invest in with things of worth (like attention, time, or money) are our Governing Values.

The principles on which we bet our actions in the future are those we have faith in; they are Our Beliefs.

Some people even have this written on their window.

The Belief Window Defines Our Limits and Sets Our Capabilities

The three stories that follow illustrate how our windows define our behavior and influence how we make decisions and how we relate to other people:

12

The Hypnotized Singer

A few years ago, I was astonished by what I saw at one of those traveling hypnotist shows. One particular little man volunteered to be hypnotized and was first asked to sing. His voice was raspy, and he hesitantly got through the song, even with the laughter of the crowd.

He was put under by the hypnotist and quietly told he was a world-famous singer about to give one of his finest performances. He was before a huge audience who had paid over $20 each just to hear him. He was then asked to sing again.

The difference was dramatic. This time, he was quite good and very pleasing to hear — not twenty dollars worth, but still much better than anticipated.

Robert's Possessions Give Him Away

My friend Robert has a need to be valued by others and seen as a person of substance and means. He drives a BMW, wears British suits and Italian shoes, and just got back from a European vacation with his Swedish wife.

The contrast between the two attempts at singing was dramatic. The only change was the writing on the man's belief window.

Robert's consistent behavior allows us to read some of the principles on his belief window. One of them seems to be: My value as a person is shown by the quality of the possessions I own. Another is: European culture and products are of the highest quality.

By knowing the principles Robert has bought, I can better understand why he does what he does without letting these things (that don't really matter to me) get in the way of our friendship.

John Loves Mary Loves John

John learned love from a family where love was given unconditionally and freely. No matter what he did, his parents still loved him. His father once said, "Even if you killed someone, we would still love you even on the electric chair."

Mary learned love from a family where love was given conditionally. These words, even if never said out loud, were always present in family relationships: "We love you if you do what we want, but we don't love you if you go against what we feel is best for you."

John and Mary got together, fell in love, and were married. They often told each other the words, "I love you." The loving words were identical, but was their meaning?

The words were the same, but was the meaning?

Sharing a Belief Window

People can often share the same window when they come together in groups. These shared windows are the commonality that binds these groups into cohesive units. Such groups can be formal or informal and can range from families to unions and from companies to nations.

Here is an example of a shared belief window that seems to be common in many businesses:

People who share a common window act, look, and think alike.

Insiders

Large windows are often held in place by wheels.

Outsider

Some other examples of organizational window sharing:

GROUP: Nazi Germany
BELIEF: Man is a creature to be bred for quality to rule the world for a 1,000-year reign.
RESULT: *During the final battles of World War II, troop trains are stopped so that trains carrying "subhumans" to the concentration camps can get through.*

GROUP: Moslem Fundamentalists
BELIEF: Allah will eventually triumph over all, and dying for the cause will take you directly to heaven.
RESULT: *Thousands of poorly trained Iranian youths die in mass attack against the Iraqi army.*

GROUP: The Rosten Family
BELIEF: You kiss those you love.
RESULT: *Two weeks after the yearly family reunion, everyone mysteriously comes down with the flu.*

GROUP: I.B.M.
BELIEF: Customer service is our primary goal.
RESULT: *"It cost more for their equipment, but their service made the difference in getting our inventory control system on line."*

How to Change What's Written on the Window

We are always striving for consistency and order, and nowhere is this more important to us than in what is written on our belief window. When two opposing principles are seen in juxtaposition to each other, we can't rest until harmony and consistency are restored. Something just has to be combined, refined, or dropped from the window to restore the order.

The psychological term for the effects of juxtaposing opposite principles is called cognitive dissonance.

Often, the simple act of seeing and comparing two opposing principles will help us choose the more correct one. Here's how it works:

The Window Changing Process

1. See the old principle.

2. Show an opposite— a principle, a situation, or a new context.

3. Choose the more correct principle or create a new principle that is consistent and not in conflict.

Let's see how the process works with a couple of examples:

Old Principle: I'm ugly!
Opposite: Paul Newman says, "You're the most beautiful woman I have ever seen."
New Principle: I am nice looking.

It is easier to see the choice when you see both the old principle and the opposite idea in one total view.

Old Principle: The government should help the poor.
Opposite: Your obnoxious neighbor who hasn't worked for years says, "Why work, honey? I can make more by doing nothing than by being silly like you and going to work every day."
New Principle: The government should only help those in real need who can't work.

What's Written on Your Belief Window?

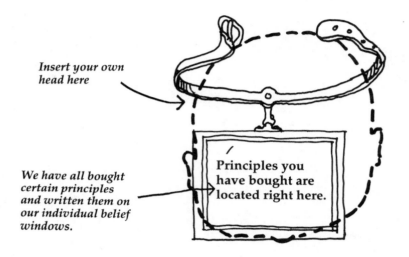

Insert your own head here

We have all bought certain principles and written them on our individual belief windows.

Principles you have bought are located right here.

We all have a belief window in front of our faces. We look through it to see the world and make sense of it. Just knowing that fact can give us a considerable amount of power, both over our own actions and in understanding the actions of others. And, seeing our own principles and the degree to which they dictate who we are and how we act can be both a severe shock and a life-changing experience.

What is written on our window defines our future.

In examining my own belief window and trying to identify the principles I've written on it, I have discovered that more than half of my principles were incorrect. My conversations with others show that percentage to be fairly well consistent across the board.

What is written on our window defines who we are, how we act, and what we may become. Our individual and group successes in life depend on our seeing life through a belief window having correct principles written on it. Incorrect principles leave us on the ground and bring us face-to-face with our nightmares; the ones that are true have enabled men and women to soar through the air and reach their dreams.

- "If I could only get control of my time, everything in my life would work out great."
- "I just can't understand my teenager. He's totally out of control."
- "We've got to get our spending under control if we're going to make it."
- "Why can't I get my employees to pull together? Who's in charge here, anyway?"
- "If we could exercise more control than our competitors over the buying process, our marketing position would improve."

THREE

Do any of these sound familiar? If so, read on. This section contains tools that can give you . . .

| Rvw | 1dy | 1wk |
| 1mo | 1qtr | 1yr |

The
Promise
of Control

Four principles and a process model that will help you achieve control in all aspects of your life.

Write down one of your current personal frustrations or problems. Chances are, it will share a common denominator with the ones on the list above; fundamentally, something is out of **control.**

We usually approach these kinds of problems in a symptomatic way: take a time management course, haul junior to the school counselor, revise the family budget again, crack down once more on those who arrive late at work. In short, we nibble at the edges rather than attack the heart of the matter: **gaining control.**

This insert focuses on the basic principles of control. It will help you understand:
- **What control is**
- **How control works**
- **How to get control**

The Four Principles of Control

Four tightly interconnected principles are critical to achieving personal control of your life.

1 The purpose of life is fulfilling inner needs.

Psychologists say that the driving force behind all human activity is the fulfillment of needs. While needs are complex and individual, they can be grouped into four basic categories:

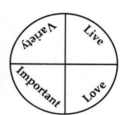

The NEEDS WHEEL shows how balance is achieved when all four needs are fulfilled in our lives.

- **We want to live.**
  No one wants to die. Even when we feel relatively safe, the desire to live manifests itself in our search for a stable job, good health, or even sound investments. Desires for safety, comfort, and security are all manifestations of our basic desire to live.

- **We want to love and be loved.**
  We go to great lengths to win love or feel that we belong. We make incredible sacrifices as spouses and friends, all because of our desire for love, both given and received.

- **We want to feel important.**
  We want people to notice and value us. We want to feel needed and respected. We search for purpose in our lives. We want to be competent in the things we do and to become more than we are now.

- **We want variety.**
  No one wants to be bored. People climb mountains, take African safaris, try new hobbies, read books, go to concerts, or take in ball games to break the routine.

2 Our fulfillment is directly related to the amount of control we feel.

The common denominator of the four basic needs is **control.** When we feel in control of our lives, we can freely give and accept love; we feel competent and capable of becoming, growing, and progressing; our lives have purpose and variety; we feel important and safe.

If we perceive that we are out of control—that events are overwhelming us and carrying us away—then we may no longer even want to live.

Control is achieved through learning and following correct principles.

3

Principles attempt to describe the natural laws governing how things work or interrelate. Scientific principles may be rather precisely defined; principles of human behavior, on the other hand, are often more generally stated and less precise. But in either case, to state a principle is to attempt to describe an apparent truth or consistent pattern.

Available scientific evidence indicates that our minds "buy" principles. Once bought, a principle is accepted as truth—even if, in reality, it is incorrect—and it then governs our outlook and actions.

In order to gain control and earn the inherent rewards, you first must identify the principles you have bought and determine whether or not they are correct. **Your success in achieving control will depend on how closely your principles match the inherent laws that govern the world as it really is.**

CORRECT PRINCIPLES	INCORRECT PRINCIPLES
enable us to achieve our goal of control	fight against our efforts to achieve control

Principles are best learned and applied through seeing and understanding relationships.

4

The principles we have bought are influenced by our needs, and they, in turn, influence our behavior and the results we achieve. These relationships can best be seen through a simple visual pattern we call the **Control Model**. In addition to showing relationships between all of the elements in the needs fulfillment equation, the Control Model points up the critical role of principles.

NEEDS	PRINCIPLES	RULES	BEHAVIOR	RESULTS
The driving force behind all of our behavior and actions.	The basic concepts we accept with respect to our needs.	A specific application of the principle.	Our actions, based on our rules and principles, to achieve desired results.	The end product. If the principles are sound, the long-term results will be also.

How the Control Model Works

Put yourself in this situation: A friend of yours comes to you, close to tears, and asks for advice with regard to a teenage son. This friend wants to have a close, loving relationship with his son, but is also deeply concerned about the possibility that peer pressure will lead the son into drug abuse, illicit sex, or worse. The father has increasingly clamped down on the son's activities, grilling him whenever he leaves the house, and giving him the third degree again when he returns, especially if the hour is later than expected. But now things seem to be getting worse. The son is avoiding his father and stays away from home whenever possible. One night, he was gone all night and couldn't offer a satisfactory excuse the next day. The father asks, "What am I doing wrong?"

Use the Control Model to see what's happening:

1. *First look at the father's behavior and try to determine what needs he is seeking to fulfill and the principles he has bought in relation to them.*

2. *What need is behind this behavior? Referring to the four basic needs, he appears to want to love his son and have that love reciprocated.*

3. *What principles has the father bought? Looking at his actions, he seems to feel he must keep a tight rein on the son so he won't get into trouble.*

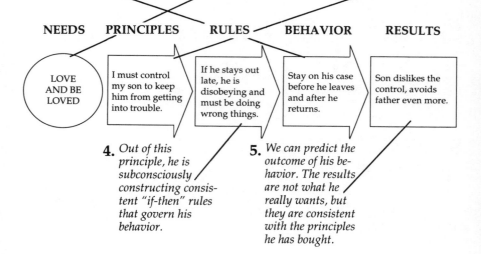

NEEDS   PRINCIPLES   RULES   BEHAVIOR   RESULTS

| LOVE AND BE LOVED | I must control my son to keep him from getting into trouble. | If he stays out late, he is disobeying and must be doing wrong things. | Stay on his case before he leaves and after he returns. | Son dislikes the control, avoids father even more. |

4. *Out of this principle, he is subconsciously constructing consistent "if-then" rules that govern his behavior.*

5. *We can predict the outcome of his behavior. The results are not what he really wants, but they are consistent with the principles he has bought.*

If you point out to this father that so far he has come up with nothing but a kid who stays away even more, he may respond that the boy needs even tighter control and needs to understand who's in charge of the family. If you suggest that he lay off so that the boy can establish some needed independence, the father will probably continue as he is doing. Generally, people do not change if you just attack their behavior. You must address a person's basic needs before you can initiate change, and then you must help the person buy new principles that will be more likely to fulfill those needs.

The key to changing principles is the process of examining alternatives (once we buy a principle, it often doesn't occur to us that there **are** alternatives). To do this, place the present principle next to an alternative one, and decide which is more correct. In this case, you might show the father this principle: **Trust is the key to any relationship.**

Try selling the father on the new principle rather than attacking his existing behavior. His basic need is to love and be loved; help him focus on the question of which principle best meets his need:

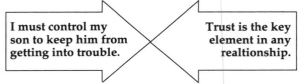

I must control my son to keep him from getting into trouble.

Trust is the key element in any realtionship.

If the father buys the new principle, everything else will fall into line. He'll set up some new "if-then" rules, and his behavior will probably focus on building trust with his son, thereby encouraging the more responsible behavior he wants to see.

Why does this change occur? Psychologists tell us that the mind automatically seeks to resolve "cognitive dissonance" or the inner conflict that occurs when two opposing beliefs or principles try to exist in the mind at the same time. A choice between the principles must be made to restore inner harmony. Clearly seeing the choices helps a person in making the right one, exercising control.

NEEDS	PRINCIPLES	RULES	BEHAVIOR	RESULTS

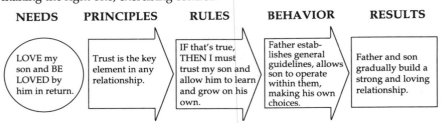

LOVE my son and BE LOVED by him in return.

Trust is the key element in any relationship.

IF that's true, THEN I must trust my son and allow him to learn and grow on his own.

Father establishes general guidelines, allows son to operate within them, making his own choices.

Father and son gradually build a strong and loving relationship.

The Control Model Also Works in Business

Businesses have needs, too.

Not only is the Control Model a powerful tool for achieving control and success in your personal life, but the basic principles around which it is built apply equally well to businesses and organizations.

The four basic human needs have their counterparts in the business world.

- **Businesses also want to live (or be VIABLE, in business terms).** Security in a business environment is essential.

- **Love is not exactly a business need, but a close cousin, RESPECT, is.** In order for a business to succeed, it must achieve a reputation of competency.

- **A business also wants to be important, to have COMPETITIVE IMPACT.** It needs a reason for people to buy its goods or services. This is closely related to the concept of MARKET NICHE.

- **The need for INNOVATION and CREATIVITY is the business counterpart of the human need for variety.** This ongoing need encourages growth and progression; those businesses who stand still are soon passed by the competition.

The BUSINESS NEEDS WHEEL has many parallels with the wheel of human needs.

An Illustration: Of Tubes and Transistors

In 1947, the transistor was invented by Bell Laboratories, the research arm of AT&T. Almost immediately, it could be seen that the transistor would replace the bulkier, more expensive, and less reliable vacuum tubes that were the key components in any radio or television set.

The strange thing is that nobody did anything about it—at least not in America. The leading American manufacturers were proud of their Super Heterodyne radio sets, which were the ultimate in craftsmanship and quality. These manufacturers announced that, while they were looking at the transistor, it "would not be ready" until "sometime around 1970."

Sony was practically unknown outside Japan at that time and was not even involved in consumer electronics. But Sony's president, Akio Morita, saw the potential of the transistor and quietly bought a license from Bell Laboratories to use the transistor for the ridiculous sum of $25,000. Within two years, Sony produced the first portable transistor radio—an inexpensive model that weighed only one-fifth as much as a comparable vacuum tube radio. With prices that were only one-third that of vacuum tube radios, Sony captured the entire United States market for cheap radios by the early 1950s, and within five years the Japanese had captured the world market as well.

Why did the American manufacturers behave this way? The Control Model provides some useful insights.

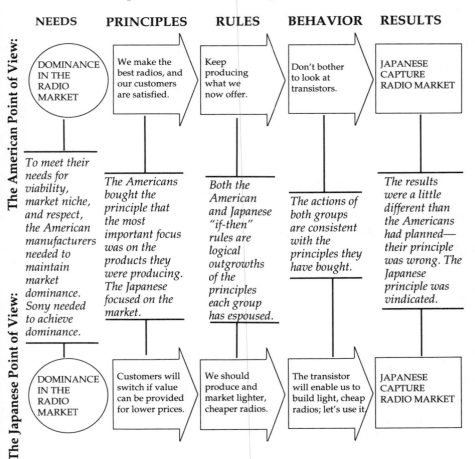

Who achieved control? The people with the correct principles.

Try it!

Once you've identified the principles on which you (or others) are operating, identified the available alternatives, and made a conscious choice, you are on the way to gaining control.

A. Identify the Principles That Have Been Bought

1. *Start with behaviors or actions that are evident in the situation. Try to identify them clearly and concisely.*

2. *Ask: "What basic need does this action or behavior seem aimed at fulfilling?"*

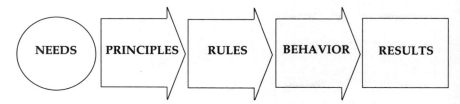

3. *Ask: "What principle has been bought here?" The principle needs to be consistent with both the behavior and the need it seeks to address.*

4. *Ask: "Do I see any 'if-then' rules that have been derived from this principle?" Again, such rules will be suggested by the behavior or action.*

5. *Finally, ask: "Has this chain of principles, rules, and actions produced results that satisfy the need?" If not, the principle is probably incorrect.*

B. Compare Principles and Determine Which Is Best

Write out your description of a principle that has been bought, then look for any other principles applicable to this situation that might be more successful as a basis for action. Often, just seeing an incorrect principle next to a more correct one will help you see the best choice.

C. Project the Results of Using Alternative Principles

Once you've identified the need you're trying to address, it's a simple matter to "plug in" other principles and project results. This will help you identify the best principle on which to base action in situations where many principles seem applicable and appropriate.

Task Mapping is a planning tool. It breaks the steps of accomplishing a task into a visual schematic or map, making scheduling, assigning resources, and plotting progress much easier. Here is a light-hearted introduction to this project-management process.

FOUR

Rvw	1dy	1wk
1mo	1qtr	1yr

How Do You Eat An ELEPHANT?

Everyone knows the answer to that question —one bite at a time. But how does one reduce the elephant into those bite-size pieces?

The following pages examine the process of Task Mapping, a planning tool to help break our elephants into more palatable pieces, to organize the immense and seemingly endless assignments we receive daily into smaller sizes that are easier to manage.

STEPS TO TASK MAPPING

Today's managers face a proliferation of "elephants." Massive and important, they are dropped on managers' desks late Friday afternoon and are expected to be meticulously dissected, carefully prepared, and ready to eat on Monday morning. Task Mapping, a proven recipe for dividing elephants into digestible pieces, will teach you to organize long-range or short-term tasks so that they are easier to place, better managed, and ultimately more consumable.

1: END FIRST

This may look like the end result of your task map on how to eat an elephant.

While it may sound strange, the recipe for task mapping begins by visualizing the end results first; in other words, seeing the elephant in its ready-to-eat stage. How does it smell, look, and taste? Will you serve elephant steak or stew? of the African, Indian, or Asiatic variety? Where and when will you serve it? How many will partake of the delicacy? Will you need recipe copies for possible purchasing agents, or are you planning simply to freeze it as a solution to the rise in meat prices?

To visualize the end results, you must be able to project into the future the definition and exact details of the desired outcome.

2: TIME LINE

Putting time constraints on your task makes it more realistic and helps you see the inherent problems and possibilities involved in accomplishing the task.

Next, estimate how much time the entire process will take—for example, from obtaining and preparing an elephant to washing dishes after eating it. This figure should be put on a visible time line. This time line will vary depending on the project to be accomplished. For instance, if elephants live in your backyard, your time line will be much shorter than it will be for someone who must schedule a safari to Africa to find an animal. This figure is only a projected estimate, and the time line may change and evolve as you follow your own task-mapping process.

3: CHUNKS

Breaking the entire project into big chunks is the next step. Divisions exist in any process, so watch for the natural crack lines. For example, after eating dinner, we stand up from the table and do the dishes. After quartering a carcass, a butcher naturally begins to section the quarters. Not all tasks have such obvious crack lines, but when a change in function occurs while you are accomplishing a task, identify each distinct function as a separate chunk.

Follow the natural crack lines to break the huge project into smaller and smaller pieces.

Failure to dissect a project into large chunks can cause confusion and poor performance. For instance, one boss, who had been without a secretary for six weeks, immediately put her new secretary to work. "Start there," she said, pointing to an immense, unorganized mass of paper. Unaware of any natural crack lines or chunks, the secretary began "gulping" up the piles. The first hour was disastrous—the following two, worse. At the end of the day, the boss met with her assistants. "I'm afraid we've made a big mistake," she said. "This secretary is totally incompetent."

The boss would have seen dramatically different results had she given some hints as to the natural crack lines: "Divide this mess into accounts payable, accounts receivable, and general correspondence," she could have said. The secretary's work, no doubt, would have progressed in a more efficient manner.

4: SEQUENCE

The fourth step in Task Mapping is arranging the big chunks in a sequential order. If, in your own project, two or more large chunks must be accomplished at the same time, just place them at the same point on the time line. For instance, the secretary could have begun with the accounts payable, then moved onto the accounts receivable. Or, after prioritizing each pile by arranging it in chronological order, she could have worked on the piles concurrently.

All tasks can be put in sequential order of accomplishment, even though some steps may be done simultaneously.

HOW TO EAT AN ELEPHANT

Here is a possible task map used in developing our plan for eating an elephant:

YEARS

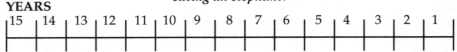

| 15 | 14 | 13 | 12 | 11 | 10 | 9 | 8 | 7 | 6 | 5 | 4 | 3 | 2 | 1 |

The time line may vary depending on the work to be accomplished.

The **PREPARATION AND CONSUMPTION** chunk is a set cycle that repeats itself until the elephant is all gone.

Based on the average family's consumption of meat per year and the amount of elephant available, it is going to take fifteen years to finish this whole project.

I CAN'T BELIEVE I ATE THE WHOLE THING!

Monthly, the meat is brought monthly to the home freezer. Space is limited.

Eaten ◀ Served ◀ Cooked ◀ Thawed ◀ Selected

Rotate Menus

Weekly, the recipes must be selected and meals planned. Planning too far in advance can cause trouble. You need to fit the continually changing human element into the plan.

END HERE!

The **SELECTION** chunk is where the menus are selected and meals planned.

Since he did such a good job on the elephant, I think I'll give him a hippo next.

Beware of the boss who wants to give you more things than you can sink your teeth into.

The big secret to this entire technique is organizing everything backwards. When you communicate the plan to someone else, just reverse the order.

THE BIG SECRET

DAYS

7 6 5 4 3 2 1

24 HOURS

There isn't much time here!

START HERE!

This is going to take a week.

The **PROCESSING** chunk involves freezing the elephant. It needs to be preserved during the time needed to do the subsequent steps.

The **PREPARATION** chunk is where it's cut up and shipped to the packing plant to be frozen. Time is critical here.

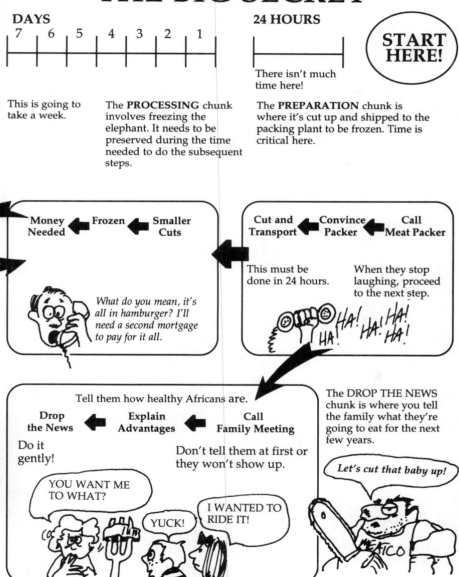

Money Needed ← **Frozen** ← **Smaller Cuts**

What do you mean, it's all in hamburger? I'll need a second mortgage to pay for it all.

Cut and Transport ← **Convince Packer** ← **Call Meat Packer**

This must be done in 24 hours.

When they stop laughing, proceed to the next step.

HA! HA! HA! HA! HA!

Tell them how healthy Africans are.

Drop the News ← **Explain Advantages** ← **Call Family Meeting**

Do it gently!

Don't tell them at first or they won't show up.

YOU WANT ME TO WHAT?

YUCK!

I WANTED TO RIDE IT!

The DROP THE NEWS chunk is where you tell the family what they're going to eat for the next few years.

Let's cut that baby up!

Divide each large chunk into smaller chunks, breaking the larger pieces into a size that you can get your teeth into.

5: SHIFT SMALLER

Repeat steps 3 and 4 with the existing chunks. Divide every large chunk into smaller chunks. Prepare a list of all tasks that need to be accomplished with each large chunk. Write them on individual slips of paper for quick adjustments. In scaling down, you may want to consider the following:

- What are the relationships between the tasks? Drawing arrows between tasks shows the best sequence.
- Are the tasks sequential (one after the other) or must any or all of them be done simultaneously?
- Who should accomplish each task?
- What is the longest time line that has been defined? Can it be accomplished in the time required by the final deadline?

Shifting to smaller and smaller chunks will allow you to really sink your teeth into the tasty morsels.

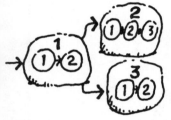

Place the small chunks in sequential order inside the large chunks.

6: LAYOUT

Starting with the last big chunk, lay out every big chunk in sequential order from the end to the beginning. Then, lay out the small chunks in sequential order and place them inside the large chunks to which they belong. Because you have worked backward, when all pieces are placed, you could have a backwards task map. Now, flip-flop the whole map so that it reads from beginning to end. Now you are ready to put the map in its final form, such as the schematic or report.

FINE POINTS OF TASK MAPPING

- Keep all the chunks on separate pieces of paper for flexibility in arranging the time line.
- The entire process is evolutionary. The time line will need adjusting right up until the end.
- If you can't extract bite-size chunks from the project, problems may be inherent in the task.
- Draw arrows to show relationships between tasks and the direction of activity.

The fine points of task mapping will help you simplify the process.

FOR EXAMPLE

Don had been a "gulper" all his life, consuming entire tasks at work in one bite. Once he learned how to eat an elephant, however, he was a changed man. The following is a brief excerpt of his life, before and after the insight.

Excessive gulping gave Don severe acid indigestion.

BEFORE Don's planning approach of the past

AFTER Don's approach to planning now

Friday afternoon at 4:45 p.m., J.P. hands Don a planning job.	Friday afternoon at 4:45 p.m., J.P. hands Don a planning job.

PANIC!

"What should I do?" Don chants. Groping in the dark, eyes dilated, and tongue hanging out, he runs wildly.

Don haphazardly flings things together. Last-minute loose ends dominate his process; the clock ticks away.

Incredibly, he makes the deadline and presents the plan Monday morning. Everybody has a great time poking fun at it.

QUIET CONFIDENCE

Don is calm, in charge, and under control. Task mapping begins.

The process is rough at first. The chunks are selected, placed, then divided again and laid out.

The map takes a definite shape—almost by itself.

The map is reversed and neatly placed in graph form for Monday's meeting.

He finished early and lets the plan and his mind sit for a day!

Well!?

Great!

MAPPING:
An Effective Planning Tool

No matter the size of your project, if you apply the task-mapping tool, your time will be used more productively. Managing tasks will cease to be painful and will become a pleasant challenge. This section of the booklet was created by using the following task map.

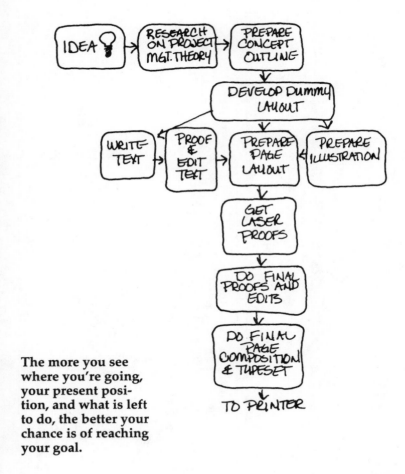

The more you see where you're going, your present position, and what is left to do, the better your chance is of reaching your goal.

A task map will give you direction, allow you to assess your progress every step, and even remind you of necessary deadlines so that nothing slips by forgotten.

FIVE

Six Steps To Building The
Productivity Pyramid

You're alone, it's 3:00 in the morning, and you can't sleep—questions won't stop forming in your mind. What do you really want? Whom do you want to be? When have you felt the magic? How can you feel it again?

Has this ever happened to you? Life is going along smoothly, just how you usually like it. But inside you feel a nagging, aching something. One day while thinking alone, you suddenly feel the ache of knowing what you could have accomplished or could be doing. You see the disparity between what you are and what you really want to be.

Your dreams may seem unreal and unattainable. How could you ever reach them?

Too many of us suppress these feelings, not knowing how to reach our dreams. Thus, we may, as Thoreau said, "lead lives of quiet desperation."

There is a way to escape this. In early centuries, when man wanted to get closer to the stars, he built towers. It **is** possible to build your way out of a comfort zone to inner peace. The structure to build is the Productivity Pyramid, and inner peace is its pinnacle.

Step 1: Leave the Comfort Zone

As noted by Dr. James W. Newman, each of us lives within "comfort zones"—geographical, situational, or emotional areas in which we feel comfortable and at ease. Although we don't notice it, we rarely, if ever, leave our particular comfort zones. Everyone's comfort zones are different. A typical comfort zone looks something like this:

There can be a lot of activity within the comfort zone, but no real progress results.

1 **The first step is to get up from that old rocking chair! The *decision* to break free in itself gives you more strength.**

Some efforts approach the edge of the comfort zone, but few take us beyond it.

It's Easier to Stay

Staying within your comfort zone is easy. It requires little effort beyond the usual activities. For example, a salesman had been working the same territory for fifteen years. He was making a good living and was happy with it. He had been working with the same clients for a long time and knew them well. He knew what they needed and when, and he always provided it.

Then his territory was split nearly in half. He continued to service the clients that remained in his small area, but complained bitterly to family and friends about how unfair it was that his biggest clients had been "stolen." Yet he never added new clients. He had never been very good at prospecting; it was easier to hope that business with his present clients would increase.

It's Comfortable to Stay

It feels good to be in a comfort zone. That's why we get such warm feelings when visiting a childhood home or rereading a favorite novel or returning home from a long vacation. These are good, wonderful feelings. But they can work to our detriment if we are trying to reach something that lies outside the comfort zone.

"I have no need for computers," scoffed an acquaintance who owns a small shipping house. "I have run this business successfully for thirty years without a computer, and I don't need one now! And besides that, you can't teach an old dog new tricks." That year, a new competitor stole a significant chunk of this man's business because they could provide faster service. The man retired without reaching his lifelong financial goal.

Leaving or Staying: The Cost

As shown above, you pay a price for remaining in a comfort zone: frustration, restlessness, and dissatisfaction, for example. You also pay a price for leaving a comfort zone. Whatever you decide, you must be willing to pay the price. The following statements are typical of people who are not willing to pay the price to leave the comfort zone:

Leaving a comfort zone exacts a high price—but so does staying there!

"I haven't begun to build my Pyramid. I'm not sure I want to know myself that well."

"I feel little need to do my Productivity Pyramid because I am comfortable with my life as it is."

Overcoming the Temptation to Stay

People always resist leaving a comfort zone. It doesn't happen overnight. However, you can **build** your way out. If you are constructing an office building, you start with a foundation, then build the upper levels successively. In the same way, to break out of a comfort zone, begin with a foundation and build up step by step.

Step 2: Choose Your Values

The next step, and often the hardest, is to identify **values**. We hear such comments as: "I don't know what I want," or, "It takes too much time to figure out what my values are." Identifying values seems like a colossal task—but maybe we can simplify it.

To determine your Governing Values, ask yourself, "What do I really want?"

Governing Values are the foundation of your Productivity Pyramid. To determine your Governing Values, ask, "What do I **really** want?" Imagine your ideal self. How do you want to act, feel, think? See it clearly in your mind, then write about it. This is your floor plan, and with it you can break ground.

Read over your description and extract the values it includes. What roles do family, career, health, etc., play in the description of your ideal self? Ask yourself, What values need to be espoused in order to become my ideal self? Look carefully and deeply—you may discover many implied values, such as integrity, sincerity, humility, etc.

2 **Decide what is most important to you. This will become your foundation.**

Values

You can't climb out unless you have something to hold on to.

After extracting your values, explain briefly what each means **to you.** Express your personal ideas and desires. After going through the value identification process, one man wrote:

"All my life I had tried to be a farmer like my father. When I identified my values, I finally realized, after twenty years, that I'm not a farmer! At last I could admit that carrying on the family farm was not as important to me as pursuing my own interests. Now I'm in sales and enjoy not only personal but also financial fulfillment."

What Needs to Change?

By now, you are probably seeing a difference between your ideal and present self. These feelings can be discouraging; why do we find ourselves acting in opposition to our deepest desires? There's more to it than meets the eye.

There are two underlying, subconscious components that govern our behavior: **needs** and **principles**. Everything we do is to fill one or more of four basic **needs**: to live, to love and be loved, to feel important, and to have variety. **Principles,** correct or incorrect, are rules of behavior that we believe will fill our needs. We **never** act inconsistently with our principles.

Patterns of behavior will point toward the principles you've bought.

To discover principles, look at **patterns** of behavior. Search for the common principle that underlies your actions. This part is difficult and often painful, but can bring forth the greatest personal growth.

- A talented young woman often felt that she could achieve great things, but something was holding her back. When she listed her patterns of behavior, she could see her principle: *It is better to not try than to fail.* The years of frustration came into focus, and she understood that, until she changed that principle, she would never change her behavior.

- A friend's father has been very successful in his career. To achieve his success he put some of his personal interests aside to provide his family with what he thought were the good things in life. His estranged daughter, now grown, confessed to him that what she had really wanted was *time* with him. But he couldn't understand her dissatisfaction with their relationship. After all, he had given her the best of everything. She realized sadly that he sacrificed family relationships in order to provide material things.

  Perhaps his principle was, *The best way to show love to my family is to give them nice things.* His need was probably *to love and be loved.* Did he get the love he wanted? Is his principle correct or incorrect?

Inner peace results when behavior is based on correct principles.

Step 3: Identify Long-Range Goals

Once the foundation of values is established and correct principles identified, goal setting becomes a process of determining specifically how you plan to achieve your values and apply them to your daily life.

A long-range goal is a concrete expression of your values. It brings a future event into present focus. Sometimes long-range goals are like dangling carrots—they are always just ahead of us; we never seem to get any closer. Below are two keys to overcoming this.

Goal setting is a process of determining specifically how you plan to achieve your values and apply them daily.

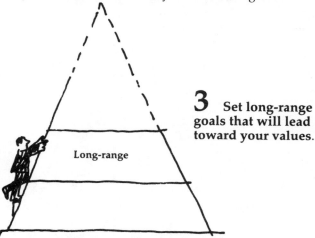

3 Set long-range goals that will lead toward your values.

Long-range

- **Write down your goals.** There is something magic about writing goals down—it solidifies the commitment you have made to yourself. Studies show that you are four times as likely to achieve a goal if you write it down.

- **Make goals specific and measurable.** Set deadlines and make your goals achievable. A goal such as *I will be in good physical condition* is just a wish because you can never measure it or know when you have achieved it!

Jim, an executive in a growing advertising agency, decided that good health was an important value. Jim's long-range goal became: *I will lower my cholesterol level by x amount by May 30.* His goal is specific (lowering his cholesterol level) and measurable (by x amount by May 30). Jim would know on May 30 whether or not he had achieved his goal.

Step 4: Set Intermediate Goals

Intermediate goals are the basic steps that lead to accomplishment of a long-range goal. If your long-range goal is to start your own company, an intermediate goal would be to find investors by a certain date. This is not a task that can normally be done in one day—it's an intermediate step. Remember these two keys:

- **Break down long-range goals into smaller tasks.** How do you eat an elephant? One bite at a time.

- **Evaluate progress periodically.** How effective are your intermediate goals in achieving the long-range goal?

To meet the goal of lowering his cholesterol level, Jim set the following intermediate goals: *Until March 30, I will (1) eliminate all fats and eat only fruit for desserts and snacks; and (2) eat no more than two eggs per week.*

On March 30, Jim and his doctor evaluated the effectiveness of these intermediate goals and together modified them in order to meet the May deadline.

Applying the above four keys to effective goal setting, Jim found great satisfaction in working toward and achieving his goals.

4 Set intermediate goals that lead to reaching the long-range goal.

Step 5: Work Toward Goals Each Day

The remaining challenge is to work toward your goals and values every day with small, manageable tasks. Jim recorded in his Day Planner what he ate each day. When he followed his diet, he put a check mark next to *control cholesterol* on his Daily Task List. Here are other suggestions for working daily toward values and goals:

- On a sticky note attached to your Pagefinder , write the values and goals you want to work on. Plan on your Daily Task List at least one task leading toward them.

- Review values and goals daily during your Planning and Solitude time. Include one task daily or weekly relating to these values.

- Reserve a special section of the Daily Task List for those tasks relating to values and goals.

5 The next step is to work toward values and goals with small, daily tasks.

Step 6: Reach the Pinnacle of Inner Peace

6 Inner peace can be achieved and maintained through steady, conscientious efforts to attain that which is of greatest value to us.

Letters from those who have built their Productivity Pyramid illustrate the power of this process.

"I cannot tell you what an impact the pyramid of values has had on my life. I know where I'm going and why."

The Productivity Pyramid offers the strength and direction needed to break out of your comfort zone to achieve inner peace.

"The result is renewed self-confidence, higher self-esteem, a greater sense of accomplishment and personal fulfillment, and most importantly, peace of mind."

"You were right in asking, 'Am I willing to pay the price?' in leaving my comfort zone. I discovered that it is well worth it."

"Doing the pyramid has put life's activities into perspective."

"I am amazed at what I am learning about myself as I ponder my values. I know what I want from life now, and for the first time, I see a tangible vehicle to reach my goals and bring my life in line with my values. It is exciting!"

Would You Like to Learn More?

If you would like a more in-depth look at other aspects
of personal productivity, you'll want to read:

Gaining Control: Your Key to Freedom and Success
by Robert F. Bennett
with Kurt Hanks and Gerreld L. Pulsipher

The principles presented in this book will help you solve
problems more effectively, make better personal or management
decisions, and more successfully deal with difficult business
or family relationships. Includes examples of how to use the
Control Model in a wide variety of situations.

Hardcover	#5518	$13.95
Paperback	#5533	$7.95

Time Management: An Introduction to the Franklin System
by Richard I. Winwood

In this book you will find profound insights that unlock personal
energies for achievement, ways to discover your hidden
potential, and the proven time management techniques taught
in Franklin Quest seminars.

Hardcover	#5537	$13.95

You can order these and other Franklin products conveniently
and quickly by calling toll free 1-800-654-1776 or by writing to:

Franklin Quest Co.
P.O. Box 25127
Salt Lake City, Utah 84125-0127

NOTES

NOTES

NOTES